Images & Insights from the Song of Solomon

Our Song

Meditations on
Love & Marriage

Images & Insights from the Song of Solomon

Our Song

Meditations on Love & Marriage

HOLMAN
BIBLE PUBLISHERS

NASHVILLE, TENNESSEE

OUR SONG
Copyright © 2001
Broadman & Holman Publishers
Nashville, Tennessee

ISBN 1-58640-011-8

All Scripture quotations are taken from the
HOLMAN CHRISTIAN STANDARD BIBLE
© Copyright 2001 by Holman Bible Publishers

Printed in Belgium
1 2 3 4 04 03 02 01

What is your picture of marriage?

Arm-in-arm down the church aisle, oblivious to the organ music and camera flashes? Summer picnics? Quiet evenings? Beach vacations? Or is it a retired couple shopping for hose and after-shave at the drug store, stopping for ice cream on the way home, and crooning to an old song on the AM radio?

Yes, yes. It is all of those things, yes, and everything in between. Every moment, every word, every wink and glance. Every Tuesday, every paycheck, every early morning alarm.

In sharing life with another in the covenant of marriage, the ordinary becomes holy. The simple becomes ceremonious. The daily becomes significant.

Aren't God's gifts always like that?

This book is a reminder that God takes delight in marriage. In all of it. Why else would He include love poetry like the Song of Solomon in the Scriptures—ancient writings full of unabashed language and overt sexual themes that can make even the most serious Bible reader blush?

God is not embarrassed by what is pure, nor the least bit afraid that any imitation will ever deliver pleasures more rich and fulfilling than those of seeking love's desire in the only place it can be found—in the eyes, the arms, the heart of your lifelong companion.

In Christian marriage, romance doesn't have to be shushed behind God's back. Sex and sanctification can snuggle up in the same sentence. It is all part of celebrating what God has given, becoming one with another while simultaneously pursuing purity and holiness.

That's why the Song of Solomon (or the Song of Songs, as we prefer to call it) is so important. Could the Bible truly be complete and adequate for Christian life if it only spoke of sexuality in terms of prohibitions, restraints, and dangers, without giving us a positive picture of healthy love? Would God give us a gift so potentially wonderful and rewarding, yet practically ensure that we mishandle it by leaving us no instructions on how to express it unselfishly and enjoy it passionately? God wants to teach and empower us to live our married lives in pure devotion to one another and with a singular commitment to Jesus Christ. And they can both be done— all at the same time—from the very beginning of marriage, through its frightfully busy and demanding years, to its golden days. Even on its most ordinary of days.

So whether you're nearing marriage, just beginning, or already have years of experience, let this book call you to the highest ideals of fidelity and commitment— and as a result, to the unequaled blessings of discovering love in one…and only one.

Admittedly, the Song of Songs is not easy to understand. Many interpret it in different and perhaps equally correct ways. On each page in this book, which divides the complete text into short, running segments, you will find an idea of what the Scripture seems to be saying, as well as a classic quotation to reinforce its meaning.

But remember—the Song does not flow like acts in a play. It is simply a love song in two parts: the man's and the woman's, assisted by a backdrop of choruses—usually a group of young women, at one point the brothers of a young girl. You'll see their names listed as speakers to help you follow along, though even this detail is not easy to ascribe with absolute certainty. When the speaker's identity is in question, it appears in parentheses.

How handsome

Discovering Love

How beautiful you are,
my darling,
How very beautiful!
Your eyes are doves.

you are, my love,
How delightful!

I wish I could remember the first day,

first hour, first moment, of your meeting me,

If bright or dim the season, it might be

Summer or Winter for aught I can say;

So unrecorded did it slip away,

So blind was I to see and to foresee,

So dull to mark the budding of my tree

That would not blossom yet for many a May.

If only I could recollect it, such

A day of days! I let it come and go

As traceless as a thaw of bygone snow;

It seemed to mean so little, meant so much;

If only now I could recall that touch,

First touch of hand in hand—Did one but know!

Christina Rossetti

The Song of Songs
Chapter 1

The woman begins the song with a heartfelt wish that the man she loves would come to her, that he would reciprocate her love for him.

1 Solomon's Finest Song

Woman

2 O that he would kiss me with the kisses of his mouth!

For your love is more delightful than wine.

3 The fragrance of your perfume is intoxicating;

your name is perfume poured out.

No wonder young women adore you.

4a Take me with you—let us hurry.

O that the king would bring me to his chambers.

"*You have entered young womanhood, and will perhaps be asked to give your life* into the keeping of some man. Remember that I have thought about you and longed for you that you may find another soul who will love you better than himself and whom you can love better than anything else in the world, and who will be grand and noble in every way. It will not matter so much if he is poor, if only he loves you better than himself and is worthy of your love. Never marry anyone for a home, or a chance to have your own way. There will be no happiness in it. Do not marry anyone to whom you cannot look up and give honor next to God. Unless you can marry such a man, it is better not to marry at all."

Grace Livingston Hill

A chorus of Jerusalemite young women now join the song, echoing the woman's sentiments. Everyone can see what a wonderful man he is.

Young Women

4b We will rejoice and be glad for you;

we will praise your love more than wine.

Woman

It is only right that they adore you.

If thou must love me, let it be for nought
Except for love's sake only. Do not say
"I love her for her smile—her look—her way
Of speaking gently—for a trick of thought
That falls in well with mine, and verily brought
A sense of pleasant ease on such a day."
For these things in themselves, Beloved, may
Be changed, or change for thee; and love, so wrought,
May be unwrought so. Neither love me for
Thine own dear pity's wiping my cheeks dry;
A creature might forget to weep, who bore
Thy comfort long, and lose thy love thereby!
But love me for love's sake, that evermore
Thou mayst love on, through love's eternity.

Elizabeth Barrett Browning

The thought of his gaze almost frightens her, for she has dark, weather-worn skin. Will he look deep enough to see her true beauty?

Woman

5 O daughters of Jerusalem,

I am dark like the tents of Kedar,

yet lovely like the curtains of Solomon.

6 Do not stare at me because I am dark,

for the sun has gazed on me.

My mother's sons were angry with me;

they made me a keeper of the vineyards.

My own vineyard I have not kept.

As I stand on this side of matrimony, I still have so many questions. Will I know when I'm walking through the story for the first time? Will I recognize the event that will begin the chapters of my love story with my mate? Will time stand still for one moment to tell me that this person—this one person, out of all the billions bustling on the planet—is the one? Will I realize when it happens? Or might I miss it?… How will you respond when one day you look on your love story? Will it bring back tears of joy or tears of remorse? Will it remind you of God's goodness or your lack of faith in that goodness? Will it be a story of purity, faith, and selfless love? Or will it be a story of impatience, selfishness, and compromise? It's your choice. Write a love story with your life that you'll feel proud to tell.

Joshua Harris

The Song of Songs
Chapter 1

Where can she find him? The man advises her to look for him among the sheep. She shouldn't hesitate to find the man she loves.

Woman

7 Tell me, you whom I love:

Where do you pasture your sheep?

Where do you let them rest at noon?

Why should I be like one who veils herself

beside the flocks of your companions?

Man

8 If you don't know for yourself,

most beautiful of women,

follow the tracks of the flock,

and pasture your young goats

near the shepherds' tents.

$\mathscr{S}$end me some token, that my hope may live,

$\mathscr{O}$r that my easeless thoughts may sleep and rest;

Send me some honey to make sweet my hive,

That in my passion I may hope the best.

I beg no ribbon wrought with thine own hands

To knit our loves in the fantastic strain

Of new-touched youth; nor a ring to show the stands

Of our affection, that as it's round and plain,

So should our loves meet in simplicity.

No, nor the coralls which thy wrist infold,

Laced up together in congruity,

To show our thoughts should rest in the same hold;

No, nor thy picture, though most gracious,

And most desired, because best like the best;

Nor witty lines, which are most copious,

Within the writings which thou hast addressed.

Send me nor this, nor that, to increase my store,

But swear that thou thinkest I love thee, and no more.

John Donne

Ah, yes! Her love is returned. She has caught his eye, as though she were the richly adorned mare that pulls Pharaoh's chariot.

Man

9 I compare you, my darling,

to a mare among Pharaoh's chariots.

10 Your cheeks are beautiful with jewelry—

your neck with its necklace.

11 We will make gold jewelry for you,

accented with silver.

It's easy to mistake romance for love, yet there are many differences.

Romance is an eager striving always to appear attractive to each other. Love is two people who find beauty in each other no matter how they look.

Romance is the anguish of waiting for the phone to ring to bring you a voice that will utter endearments. Love is the anguish of waiting for a call that will assure you someone else is happy and safe.

Romance is flattering attentions. Love is genuine thoughtfulness.

Romance can't last. Love can't help it.

Marjorie Holmes

*She responds to his words with a love song of her own,
for even the air around him gives off a pleasing aroma.*

Woman

12 While the king is on his couch,

my perfume releases its fragrance.

13 My love is a sachet of myrrh to me,

spending the night between my breasts.

14 My love is a cluster of henna blossoms to me,

in the vineyards of En-gedi.

After we have surveyed, as far as possible, all the other creatures in the world,

eventually God presents us with one who is special, one who strikes a deeper chord in us than anyone else was able to do. Although the person may be very unlike us in many important ways, still there is something inside us which recognizes the other as being bone of our bone and flesh of our flesh, akin to us on a level far deeper than personality. This is a blood tie, an affinity of the heart in every sense. It is as if we discover an actual kinship with the one we love, which the marriage ceremony serves only to make official. To be married is to have found in a total stranger a near and long-lost relative.

Mike Mason

No longer are they admirers from afar. They have declared their deepest feelings face to face. Love has drawn them together.

Man

15 How beautiful you are, my darling,

how very beautiful!

Your eyes are doves.

Woman

16 How handsome you are, my love,

How delightful!

Our bed is lush with foliage;

17 the beams of our house are cedars,

and our rafters are cypresses.

Let me see your face.

Chapter 2

The Waiting Game

I charge you;
do not stir up or awaken love
until the appropriate time.

let me hear your voice.

They say there is a young lady here who is beloved of that Great Being who made and rules the world, [who] fills her mind with exceeding sweet delight, and that she hardly cares for anything except to meditate on Him. Therefore, if you present all the world before her, with the richest of its treasures, she disregards it and cares not for it, and is unmindful of any pain or affliction. She has a strange sweetness in her mind, and singular purity in her affections; is most just and conscientious in all her conduct; and you could not persuade her to do anything wrong or sinful if you would give her all the world. She will sometimes go about from place to place, singing sweetly, and seems to be always full of joy and pleasure; and no one knows for what. She loves to be alone, walking in the fields and groves, and seems to have Someone invisible always conversing with her.

Jonathan Edwards

Humbly she confesses that she is just a common flower of the field. No, he replies. She makes the others look like thornbushes.

Woman

1 I am a rose of Sharon, a lily of the valleys.

Man

2 Like a lily among thorns,

so is my darling among the young women.

Woman

3 Like an apricot tree among the trees of the forest,

so is my love among the young men.

I delight to sit in his shade,

and his fruit is sweet to my taste.

4 He brought me to the banquet hall,

and he looked on me with love.

Sometime, when all life's lessons have been
learned, and sun and stars forevermore have set,
The things which our weak judgments here have spurned,
The things o'er which we grieved with lashes wet,
Will flash before us out of life's dark night,
As stars shine most in deeper hints of blue;
And we shall see how all God's plans are right,
And how what seemed reproof was love most true.
Then be content poor heart;
God's plans, like lilies pure and white, unfold;
we must not tear the close-shut leaves apart—
Time will reveal the chalices of gold.
And if, through patient toil, we reach the land
Where tired feet, with sandals loosed, may rest,
When we shall clearly see and understand,
I think that we will say, "God knew the best!"

May Riley Smith

❦

Love has left her breathless. She desires the man of her dreams, but she must not allure him yet. Love, like all good things, must wait.

Woman

5 Sustain me with raisins;

refresh me with apricots,

for I am lovesick.

6 His left hand is under my head,

and his right hand embraces me.

7 Young women of Jerusalem, I charge you,

by the gazelles and the wild does of the field:

do not stir up or awaken love

until the appropriate time.

If unchastity in a woman, whom St. Paul terms the glory of man, be such a scandal and dishonor, then certainly in a man, who is both the image and glory of God, it must, though commonly not so thought, be much more deflowering and dishonorable; in that he sins both against his body, which is the perfecter sex, and his own glory, which is in the woman; and, that which is worst, against the image and glory of God, which is in himself.

John Milton

The man is equally lovesick. But he knows—for now—that he can only stand outside her window and wait. Their hour will come.

Woman

8 Listen! My love is approaching.

Look! Here he comes,

leaping over the mountains,

bounding over the hills.

9 My love is like a gazelle

or a young stag.

Look! He is standing behind our wall,

gazing through the windows,

peering through the lattice.

Marriage is a serious matter, yet it is often embraced with less prayer than a college exam. I feel rather certain that the chief reason a believer often enters marriage void of fervent prayer is because inherent in the asking is His right to answer us. And once we've made up our minds, a "no" or a "wait" from God is out of the question. But to marry without the blatant inclusion of Christ is to have entirely missed the point. Marriage is sacred. It was created to be the wedding portrait of Christ and His Bride hung over the blazing fireplace of judgment. A match made in Heaven, a contract signed in blood. In the bond of marriage, we are to stand at the altar of sacrifice or we're not to stand at all.

Beth Moore

The Song of Songs
Chapter 2

Finally, when the time is right, the man proposes marriage, using a delectable, springtime theme—the universal language of love.

Woman

10 My love calls to me:

Man

Arise, my darling,

Come away, my beautiful one.

11 For now the winter is past;

the rain has ended and gone away.

12 The blossoms appear in the countryside.

The time of singing has come,

and the turtledove's cooing is heard in our land.

13a The fig tree ripens its figs;

the blossoming vines give off their fragrance.

Marriage is to human relations what monotheism is to theology.

It is a decision to put all the eggs in one basket,

to go for broke, to bet all the marbles. Is there any

abandonment more pure, more supreme, than that of

putting one's entire faith in just one God, the Lord of

all, in such a way as to allow faith to have a searching

impact on every corner of one's life? On the level of

human relations, there is only one act of trust which

can begin to approach this one, and that is the decision

to believe in one other person, and to believe so

robustly as to be ready to squander one's whole life

on that one.

Mike Mason

He continues his invitation for her to come and be his forever. She needn't be insecure any longer; he has found her altogether lovely.

Man

13b Arise, my darling.

Come away, my beautiful one.

14 O my dove—in the clefts of the rock,

in the crevices of the cliff—

let me see your face,

let me hear your voice;

for your voice is sweet,

and your face is lovely.

Gather ye rosebuds while ye may,
Old Time is still a-flying;
And this same flower that smiles today,

Tomorrow will be dying.

The glorious lamp of heaven, the sun,

The higher he's a-getting,

The sooner will his race be run,

And nearer he's to setting

That age is best which is the first,

When youth and blood are warmer;

But being spent, the worse and worst

Times still succeed the former.

Then be not coy, but use your time,

And while ye may, go marry;

For, having lost but once your prime,

You may forever tarry.

Robert Herrick

*It is a time to celebrate, suggested in this reference to what was
perhaps a favorite childhood activity that often turned into a game.*

(Woman)

15 Catch the foxes for us—

the little foxes that ruin the vineyards—

for our vineyards are in bloom.

"*How last week dragged on leaden feet while I was waiting to hear from you.*

I explored all the torments of the lovelorn. I thought all kinds of things! I suffered agonies of secret pain. You see, I was waiting for the first expression, the first reassurance…. I can never be the same again. I am a different person now—praise the Lord!—and you have made all the difference. My heart is in your keeping for ever and ever. I live from now on to serve Him and to make you happy. Life can hold nothing more satisfying or more glorious than this—the joy of building with you a home that will be a temple of God, a haven and a sanctuary, a place of peace and love, of trust and joy."

Peter Marshall

Yes. She accepts. And remembering one of her first impressions
of her beloved, she basks in the glowing warmth of maturing love.

Woman

16 My love is mine and I am his;

he feeds among the lilies.

17 Before the day breaks

and the shadows flee,

turn to me, my love, and be like a gazelle

or a young stag on the divided mountains.

The day of his wedding—

Chapter 3

Wedding Day

*Who is this coming
up from the wilderness,
scented with myrrh
and frankincense?*

*the day of his heart's
rejoicing.*

Last night I saw you in my sleep:
And how your charm of face was changed!

I asked, "Some love, some faith you keep?"

You answered, "Faith gone, love estranged."

Whereat I woke—a twofold bliss:

Waking was one, but next there came

This other: "Though I felt, for this,

My heart break, I loved on the same."

Robert Browning

The Song of Songs
Chapter 3

The anticipation of her wedding day is exciting, yet not without
its share of anxiety. Night after night, she battles her thoughts.

Woman

1 In my bed at night

I sought the one I love;

I sought him, but did not find him.

2 I will arise now and go about the city,

through the streets and the plazas.

I will seek the one I love.

I sought him, but did not find him.

3 The guards who go about the city found me.

"Have you seen the one I love?" I asked them.

4a I had just passed them

when I found the one I love.

In considering our future, we were being asked to leave the planning to God.

His ultimate plan was as far beyond our imaginings as the oak tree is from the acorn's imaginings. The acorn does what it was made to do, without pestering its Maker with questions about when and how and why. We who have been given an intelligence and a will and a whole range of wants that can be set against the divine Pattern for Good are asked to believe Him. We are given the chance to trust Him when He says to us, "If any man will let himself be lost for my sake, he will find his true self."

Elisabeth Elliot

Fully aware of her inner war between desire and discretion,
she asks those around her to help her maintain her virtue.

Woman

4b I held on to him and would not let him go

until I brought him to my mother's house—

to the chamber of the one who conceived me.

5 Young women of Jerusalem, I charge you,

by the gazelles and the wild does of the field:

do not stir up or awaken love

until the appropriate time.

When this man and this woman
stand before the altar and say,

"I, John, take thee, Mary," it is as if each of them
were holding his life in his hands, saying, "You take
it; I want you to have it—all of it—forever, and with
no strings attached." Later on, both of these persons
will be able to give more than they can at this
moment, but for now, think of what is received.
It is a joy, a wonder, a trust, a responsibility. A life
relationship with an unknown future has been
committed to another person. And likewise, that is
what has been received.

✒ *Robert Rodenmeyer*

The Song of Songs
Chapter 3

🌿

The day has come at last. The man she loves arrives for his bride, surrounded by an ancient aura of splendor, pomp, and royalty.

(Young Women)

6 Who is this coming up from the wilderness

like columns of smoke,

scented with myrrh and frankincense

from every fragrant powder of the merchant?

7 Look! Solomon's royal litter

surrounded by sixty warriors

from the mighty of Israel.

8 All of them are skilled with swords

and trained in warfare.

Each has his sword at his side

to guard against the terror of the night.

*M*ost gracious God, we give you thanks...for consecrating the union of man and woman in Jesus' name. By the power of your Holy Spirit, pour out the abundance of your blessing upon this man and this woman. Defend them from every enemy. Lead them into all peace. Let their love for each other be a seal upon their hearts, a mantle about their shoulders, and a crown upon their foreheads. Bless them in their work and in their companionship; in their sleeping and in their waking; in their joys and in their sorrows; in their life and in their death. Finally, in your mercy, bring them to that table where your saints feast forever in your heavenly home; through Jesus Christ our Lord, who with you and the Holy Spirit lives and reigns, one God, for ever and ever.

Book of Common Prayer

The Song of Songs
Chapter 3

The thrill of their wedding day is now upon them—for her, the day she has dreamed about; for him, the "day of his heart's rejoicing."

(Young Women)

9 King Solomon made a sedan chair for himself

with wood from Lebanon.

10 He made its posts of silver,

its back of gold, and its seat of purple.

Its interior is inlaid with love

by the young women of Jerusalem.

11 Come out, young women of Zion,

and gaze at King Solomon,

wearing the crown his mother placed on him

the day of his wedding—

the day of his heart's rejoicing.

You are absolutely

Chapter 4

Wedding Night

You have captured my heart with one glance of your eyes, with one jewel of your necklace.

beautiful, my darling.

"I wonder if you were conscious of averting your eyes when I looked straight into them. One time in particular I remember—you rolled your head clear away to look into the fire when I wanted to face you. Please don't! I like the look of you. I'm glad I love more in you than looks, so that if I went stone blind I would still love you, but your looks are not disconnected from it. Love you for love's sake only? Not exactly. For love's sake, yes, but for dozens of other things, too, not the least of which is every dear remembrance of your face. The grace of your forehead, the clearness of your eyes…"

Jim Elliot

Alone together at last, the man whispers love's delight for his
newfound bride—her tender face, her eyes, her hair, her smile.

Man

1 How beautiful you are, my darling.

How very beautiful!

Behind your veil,

your eyes are doves.

Your hair is like a flock of goats

streaming down Mount Gilead.

2 Your teeth are like a flock of newly shorn sheep

coming up from washing,

each one having a twin,

and not one missing.

She walks in beauty, as the night
Of cloudless climes and starry skies;
And all that's best of dark and bright
Meet in her aspect and her eyes:
Thus mellowed to that tender light
Which heaven to gaudy day denies.

One shade the more, one ray the less,
Had half impaired the nameless grace
Which waves in every raven tress
Or softly lightens o'er her face;
Where thoughts serenely sweet express
How pure, how dear their dwelling-place.

And on that cheek, and o'er that brow
So soft, so calm, yet eloquent,
The smiles that win, the tints that glow
But tell of days in goodness spent,
A mind at peace with all below,
A heart whose love is innocent!

Lord Byron

His analogies go beyond the obvious, even praising her beauty in military terms. She is tender, yes, but dignified. Stunning.

Man

3 Your lips are like a scarlet cord,

and your mouth is lovely.

Behind your veil,

your brow is like a slice of pomegranate.

4 Your neck is like the tower of David,

constructed in layers.

A thousand bucklers are hung on it—

all of them shields of warriors.

Only within the peculiar two-person sanctuary of marriage may some of the normal rules and taboos regarding adult nudity be disregarded or relaxed in perfect freedom of conscience. For to be naked with another person is a sort of picture or symbolic demonstration of perfect honesty, perfect trust, perfect giving and commitment, and if the heart is not naked along with the body, then the whole action becomes a lie and a mockery. It becomes an involvement in an absurd and tragic contradiction: the giving of the body but the withholding of the self.

Mike Mason

For the first time, he sees the mysteries of his bride. Their patient love is rewarded with the pure enjoyment of wedded togetherness.

Man

5 Your breasts are like two fawns,

twins of a gazelle, that feed among the lilies.

6 Before the day breaks

and the shadows flee,

I'll make my way to the mountain of myrrh

and the hill of frankincense.

7 You are absolutely beautiful, my darling,

with no imperfection in you.

All the commandments of God enjoining a man to love his wife

are nothing but so many necessities and capacities of joy. She that is loved is safe, and he that loves is joyful. The husband should nourish and cherish her; he should refresh her sorrows and entice her fears into confidence and pretty arts of rest. But it will concern the prudence of the husband's love to make the cares and evils as simple and easy as he can, by doubling the joys and acts of a careful friendship, by tolerating her infirmities (because by doing so he either cures her, or makes himself better). For there is nothing that cannot be misinterpreted; and yet if it be capable of a fair construction, it is the office of love to make it.

Jeremy Taylor

Desire enthralls him, yet proper respect forbids him from taking what must only be given. He will receive her when she is ready.

Man

8 Come with me from Lebanon, my bride—

with me from Lebanon!

Descend from the peak of Amana,

from the summit of Senir and Hermon,

from the dens of the lions,

from the mountains of the leopards.

9 You have captured my heart, my sister, my bride.

You have captured my heart

with one glance of your eyes,

with one jewel of your necklace.

How do I love thee?
Let me count the ways.

I love thee to the depth and breadth and height

My soul can reach, when feeling out of sight

For the ends of Being and ideal Grace.

I love thee to the level of everyday's

Most quiet need, by sun and candlelight.

I love thee freely, as men strive for Right;

I love thee purely, as they turn from Praise.

I love thee with the passion put to use

In my old griefs, and with my childhood's faith.

I love thee with a love I seemed to lose

With my lost saints—I love thee with the breath,

Smiles, tears, of all my life!—and, if God choose,

I shall but love thee better after death.

Elizabeth Barrett Browning

Till now, she has been to him a "locked garden and a sealed spring."
But in this sweet marriage moment, she has truly become his own.

Man

10 How delightful your love is, my sister, my bride.

Your love is much better than wine,

and the fragrance of your perfume than any balsam.

11 Your lips drip sweetness like the honeycomb,

my bride.

Honey and milk are under your tongue.

The fragrance of your garments is like

the fragrance of Lebanon.

12 My sister, my bride, is a locked garden—

a locked garden and a sealed spring.

Here in the security of marriage is the real meeting place for this man and this woman, for love is the enemy of haste. Here they have time for privacy, approval and blessing, and each other. Here they come to each other gladly and thankfully in the knitting together of two, free, whole human beings—willing to fulfill and to be fulfilled. The miracle of meeting gathers up all the tapestry of their common life: their worries and their unexpected joys, their private jokes that are no one else's business, their hopes and plans and dreams. There is no place to go; they have already arrived.

Robert Rodenmeyer

Who could ever be what she is now becoming to him? This night of heightening passion is but the beginning of a life shared in love.

Man

13 Your branches are a paradise of pomegranates

with choicest fruits,

henna with nard—

14 nard and saffron, calamus and cinnamon,

with all the trees of frankincense,

myrrh and aloes,

with all the best spices.

15 You are a garden spring,

a well of flowing water

streaming from Lebanon.

There comes a time when words fail and the tongue cannot utter what is in the heart, yet expression of some kind is an imperative necessity —indeed, without it a personal relation like that of man and woman in "one flesh" cannot continue. Part of the importance of sexual intercourse is that it affords husband and wife a medium for those mutual disclosures for which no words can be found; the senses become the channel of communication for all that lies too deep for utterance and yet must somehow be told.

Derrick Sherwin Bailey

His soft words and gentle wooings have enraptured her. She invites him to come—to come to his garden and receive its pleasures.

Woman

16 Awaken, north wind—

come, south wind.

Blow upon my garden,

and spread the fragrance of its spices.

Let my love come to his garden

and eat its choicest fruits.

This is my love,

Chapter 5

Love
in Real Life

*What makes
the one you love
better than another,
most beautiful of women?*

and this is my friend.

Couples whom he had counseled had often wondered how this young preacher would act when he finally fell in love. The idealism of Peter was no mere sentimentality, for it was rooted and grounded in the love of Christ. Indeed, every sermon Peter preached was a word drama, whose gigantic backdrop was a picture etched in bold strokes of God's age-long courtship of the human race. To the preacher, all human history was but the tale of God's tender wooing of the self-willed, stubborn hearts of men and women—a drama that culminated in the Cross. No romance could ever equal the romance of Calvary. But when, perchance, a little of the love of God spilled over into the hearts of a man and a woman—and when that love was blessed and sanctified by Christ—there was true romance, a "marriage made in heaven."

Catherine Marshall

The Song of Songs
Chapter 5

Newly wedded love is greeted by the smiles and good wishes
of the lovers' community. The old remember; the young wonder.

Man

1 I have come to my garden—my sister, my bride.

I gather my myrrh with my spices.

I eat my honeycomb with my honey.

I drink my wine with my milk.

(Young Women)

Eat, friends!

Drink! Be intoxicated with love!

Love is an act of will–listening to him when we are bored, keeping that perfectly couched comeback to ourselves, letting him win the argument over something unimportant. And love means not waiting to feel good before plunging into these unselfish acts, but is rather the decision to behave a certain way even when we don't feel like it. If we are to love as Christ commanded us, then we must be willing not to plant our feet on our side of the fence, howling self-righteous epithets to the other side, but rather to climb over the fence and see what the world looks like from the other point of view.

Leslie Williams

She realizes that part of their growing togetherness is an ongoing giving of the self, a willingness to consider the needs of another.

Woman

2 I sleep, but my heart is awake.

A sound! My love is knocking!

Man

Open to me, my sister, my darling,

my dove, my perfect one.

For my head is drenched with dew,

my hair with droplets of the night.

Try to bear patiently with the defects and infirmities of others, whatever they may be, because you also have many a fault which others must endure. If you cannot make yourself what you would wish to be, how can you bend others to your will? But God has so ordained this, that we may learn to bear with one another's burdens. Hence, we must support one another, console one another, mutually help, counsel, and advise, for the measure of every man's virtue is best revealed in time of adversity—adversity that does not weaken a man but rather shows what he is.

Thomas à Kempis

The emotional jolt of sexual union seems to have struck them both a bit differently. There is more to the sex act than mere function.

Woman

3 I have taken off my clothing.

How can I put it back on?

I have washed my feet.

How can I get them dirty?

4 My love thrust his hand through the opening,

and my feelings were stirred for him.

When the physical encounter of men and women in the intimate act of intercourse is not an expression of their total availability to each other, the creative fellowship of the weak is not reached. Every sexual relationship with built-in reservations, mental restrictions, or time limits is still part of the taking structure. It means, "I want you now but not tomorrow. I want something from you, but I don't want you." Love is limitless. Only when men and women give themselves to each other in total surrender—that is, with their whole person for their whole life—can their encounter bear full fruits.

Henri Nouwen

She wants him. They are together. All the principals are in place.
But somehow, it's as though he's not there. She feels abandoned.

Woman

5 I rose to open for my love.

My hands dripped with myrrh,

my fingers with flowing myrrh

on the handles of the bolt.

6 I opened to my love,

but my love had turned and gone away.

I was crushed that he had left.

I sought him, but did not find him.

I called him, but he did not answer.

Virgins, by a discreet marriage, should swallow down into their virginity another virginity, and devour such a life and spirit into their womb that it might make them, as it were, immortal here on earth, besides their perfect immortality in heaven. Then that virtue which otherwise would putrify and corrupt shall then be complete, and shall be recorded in Heaven and enrolled here on Earth; and the name of Virgin shall be exchanged for a far more honorable name— a Wife.

John Donne

Their union, though pleasurable, has required the loss of something the woman treasured. She needs him to be patient, to understand.

Woman

7 *The guards who go about the city found me.*

They beat and wounded me;

they took my cloak from me—

the guardians of the walls.

8 *Young women of Jerusalem, I charge you:*

if you find my love,

tell him that I am lovesick.

Love is quick, sincere, dutiful, joyous, and pleasant; brave, patient, faithful, prudent, serene, and vigorous, and it never seeks itself. For whenever we seek ourselves, we fall away from love. Love is watchful, humble, and upright; not weak, or frivolous, or directed toward vain things; temperate, pure, steady, calm, and alert in all the senses. Love is devoted and thankful to God, always trusting and hoping in him, even when it doesn't taste his sweetness, for without pain no one can live in love. A lover must willingly accept every hardship and bitterness for the sake of the beloved, and must never turn away from the beloved when misfortune comes. Whoever isn't prepared to endure everything, and to abide in the will of the beloved, is unworthy to be called a lover.

Thomas à Kempis

The Song of Songs
Chapter 5

What is so special about this man that has made her willing to painfully surrender herself to him? Is her gain worth her grief?

Young Women

9 What makes the one you love better than another,

most beautiful of women?

What makes him better than another,

that you would give us this charge?

Woman

10 My love is fit and strong,

notable among ten thousand.

When in disgrace with fortune and men's
eyes, I all alone beweep my outcast state

And trouble deaf heaven with my bootless cries

And look upon myself and curse my fate,

Wishing me like to one more rich in hope,

Featured like him, like him with friends possessed,

Desiring this man's art and that man's scope,

With what I most enjoy contented least;

Yet in these thoughts myself almost despising,

Haply I think on thee, and then my state,

Like to the lark at break of day arising

From sullen earth, sings hymns at heaven's gate;

For thy sweet love remembered such wealth brings

That then I scorn to change my state with kings.

William Shakespeare

Beginning at the top of his head, she recounts the qualities she
loves in her man, retracing the path that first attracted her to him.

Woman

11 His head is purest gold.

His hair is wavy

and black as a raven.

12 His eyes are like doves

beside streams of water,

washed in milk

and set like jewels.

Try to remember the vision that "being in love" gave you of who that person was.

You found no fault in him or her. Is it blindness to see a sinful man or woman thus? I think it is a special gift of vision, the power to see for a little while what God meant when He made that person. You find, after marriage, that the person is in fact a sinner, has flaws you never suspected. Try to remember then what the vision showed you. Thank God for it, and treat him or her with the sort of respect due one who will some day manifest most gloriously the image of God.

Elisabeth Elliot

She sees him in the vocabulary of flowering gardens and precious metals. More than strong and handsome—prized and valuable.

Woman

13 His cheeks are like beds of spice,

towers of perfume.

His lips are lilies,

dripping with flowing myrrh.

14 His arms are rods of gold

set with topaz.

His body is an ivory panel

covered with sapphires.

Much of our disillusionment with marriage stems from the fact that we've been duped into believing that good equals easy. In other words, we often assume that if something is difficult, it can't be of God. Nothing has been more difficult for Christ than the marriage to His Bride, yet Jude 24 says He'll present her to His Father with great joy! Just picture it: After all the ups and downs in the relationship, after all the marriage has cost Him, He'll act like a love-struck boy introducing his girl to his dad for the very first time. Why? Because He thinks she was worth it. On the pleasant days of marriage, gaze across at your groom and conclude he is worth it. On the difficult days of marriage, gaze up at your Groom and conclude He's worth it.

Beth Moore

Disillusionment has disappeared in the light of a new attitude.
Her love for him has carried her through this rite of passage.

Woman

15 His legs are alabaster pillars

set on pedestals of pure gold.

His presence is like Lebanon,

as majestic as the cedars.

16 His mouth is sweetness.

He is absolutely desirable.

This is my love, and this is my friend,

young women of Jerusalem.

I am my love's,

The Power of One

My dove,
my virtuous one, is unique.
Women see her
and declare her fortunate.

and my love is mine.

Above all the instances of love, let him preserve towards her an inviolable faith, and an unspotted chastity; for this is the marriage ring. It ties two hearts by an eternal band. It is like the cherubim's flaming sword, set for the guard of paradise.... Chastity is the security of love, and preserves all the mysteriousness like the secrets of a temple. Under this lock is deposited security of families, the union of affections, the repairer of accidental breaches. The locks and bars of modesty are a grace that is shut up and secured by all arts of heaven and the defense of laws, by honor and reputation, by fear and shame, by interest and high regards.

🖋 *Jeremy Taylor*

The Song of Songs
Chapter 6

❧

The Jerusalem girls now see a woman at peace with married life—
so at peace that they wonder where they can find men of their own.

Young Women

1 Where has your love gone,

most beautiful of women?

Which way has he turned?

We will seek him with you.

Woman

2 My love has gone down to his garden,

to beds of spice,

to feed in the gardens

and gather lilies.

3 I am my love's and my love is mine;

he feeds among the lilies.

With thee conversing I forget all time; all seasons and their change, all please alike.

Sweet is the breath of morn, her rising sweet, with charm of earliest birds. Pleasant the sun when first on this delightful land he spreads his orient beams on herb, tree, fruit, and flower, glistening with dew. Fragrant the fertile earth after soft showers, and sweet the coming on of grateful evening mild, then silent night with this her solemn bird and this fair moon, and these the gems of heaven, her starry train.

But neither breath of morn when she ascends with charm of earliest birds, nor rising sun on this delightful land, nor herb, fruit, flower, glistening with dew, nor fragrance after showers, nor grateful evening mild, nor silent night with this her solemn bird, nor walk by moon, or glittering starlight—without thee—is sweet.

John Milton

Likewise, the man expresses his own contentment with his bride.
Knowing her intimately has only served to kindle his desire for her.

Man

4 You are as beautiful as Tirzah, my darling,

lovely as Jerusalem,

awe-inspiring as an army with banners.

5a Turn your eyes away from me,

for they captivate me.

Shall I compare thee to a summer's day?

Thou are more lovely and more temperate.

Rough winds do shake the darling buds of May,

And summer's lease hath all too short a date.

Sometimes too hot the eye of heaven shines,

And often is his gold complexion dimmed;

And every fair from fair sometimes declines,

By chance or nature's changing course untrimmed.

But thy eternal summer shall not fade

Nor lose possession of that fair thou ow'st;

Nor shall Death brag thou wanderest in his shade,

When in eternal lines to time thou grow'st.

So long as men can breathe or eyes can see,

So long lives this, and this gives life to thee.

William Shakespeare

Repeating some of the same metaphors from their wedding night, he assures her that he can never be bored with her beauty.

Man

5b Your hair is like a flock of goats

streaming down from Gilead.

6 Your teeth are like a flock of ewes

coming up from washing,

each one having a twin,

and not one missing.

7 Behind your veil,

your brow is like a slice of pomegranate.

Not, Celia, that I juster am,
Or better than the rest!

For I would change each hour with them,

Were not my heart at rest.

But I am tied to very thee

By every thought I have;

Thy face I only care to see,

Thy heart I only crave.

All that in woman is adored

In thy dear self I find;

For the whole sex can but afford

The handsome and the kind.

Why then should I seek further store

And still make love anew?

For when change itself can give no more,

'Tis easy to be true.

Sir Charles Sedley

❧

Even in the company of royalty or the parading beauty of women chosen for their pleasing appearance, she is "unique,"one of a kind.

Man

8 *There are sixty queens*

and eighty concubines

and young women without number.

9 *But my dove, my virtuous one, is unique;*

she is the favorite of her mother,

perfect to the one who gave her birth.

Women see her and declare her fortunate;

queens and concubines also,

and they sing her praises.

In the cocoon the caterpillar must have many doubts that he will ever be able to break out, much less fly. But one day he finds himself outside his warm, safe cocoon, crawling around. Perhaps at times he even becomes a bit discouraged as he observes a beautiful butterfly high above him, wondering if he will ever be able to fly like that. The days pass, and as he faithfully crawls about—without even being aware of what is happening—his wings take flight, and he soars high above the ground where he once crawled. I doubt he is even aware he has become a butterfly. So it is with us. The Christian life is not suddenly "mounting up with wings" but day-by-day faithfulness.

Gigi Graham Tchividjian

Marriage has changed her. Everyone recognizes it. She can hardly remember what life was like before she felt this settled oneness.

(Young Women)

10 Who is this who shines like the dawn—

as beautiful as the moon,

bright as the sun,

awe-inspiring as an army with banners?

Woman

11 I came down to the walnut grove

to see the blossoms of the valley,

to see if the vines were budding

and the pomegranates blooming.

12 Before I knew it, my desire put me

among the chariots of my noble people.

Let me lay my head upon your breast and close my eyes against the light. I fain would rest.

I'm weary and the world looks sad. This worldly strife

Turns me to you! And, oh, I'm glad to be your wife.

Though friends may fail or turn aside, yet I have you.

And in your love I may abide for you are true.

My only solace in each grief, and in despair

Your tenderness is my relief. It soothes each care.

If joys of life could alienate this poor weak heart

From yours, then may no pleasure great enough to part

Our sympathies, fall to my lot. I'd ever remain

Bereft of friends, though true or not, just to retain

Your true regard, your presence bright,

through care and strife;

And, oh, I thank my God tonight I am your wife.

Author Unknown

She belongs to another now, not to the whims of her girlfriends.
"Come back, come back, O Shulammite?" Why would she want to?

Chorus

13 Come back, come back, O Shulammite!

Come back, come back, that we may look at you!

Man

Why would you look at the Shulammite,

as you would at the dance of the two camps?

I have treasured them

Chapter 7

Growing Together

O love,
with such delights!
at our doors is every delicacy—
new as well as old.

up for you, my love.

When I stop at the grocery store for milk and bread, I often buy flowers for Betsy. On one particular trip, when I reached the cashier, he joked, "What's the matter—you in the doghouse?" It would have been easy to laugh along with him and join in the joke. But I wanted him to know my marriage was important to me. Here was a chance to challenge his misconception, to sow in his mind a seed of hope about the tremendous potential of marriage. So without getting self-righteous about it, I answered, "No, I just love my wife."

✍ Gary Ricucci

Growing closer each day, they continue to share their love together.
The man, though now familiar with his wife, is no less fascinated.

Man

1 How beautiful are your sandaled feet,

O princess!

The curves of your thighs are like jewelry,

the handiwork of a master.

2 Your navel is a rounded bowl;

may it never lack mixed wine.

Your waist is a mound of wheat

surrounded by lilies.

3 Your breasts are like two fawns,

twins of a gazelle.

As I read the romantic story in the Song of Solomon and meditate on the intended richness of the marriage union—so rich that it serves as a living parable of the bond between Christ and His bride—I cannot help but think that Christian couples are shortchanging themselves when all they want from their sexual relationship is more pleasure and less frustration. I am not suggesting that we pursue some sort of "spiritualized sex" untouched by sheer sensual pleasure, but I do believe our sexual make-up equips us to enjoy much more than that. To splash about in a puddle when God provides an ocean is no noble self-denial; it is worse than foolish. It not only robs us of intended blessing, but robs God of glory and the joy of giving.

Larry Crabb

He cannot adequately express how deeply she moves him. What a wonder, what a blessing that love comes "with such delights!"

Man

4 *Your neck is like a tower of ivory,*

your eyes like pools in Heshbon

by the gate of Bath-rabbim.

Your nose is like the tower of Lebanon

looking toward Damascus.

5 *Your head crowns you like Mount Carmel,*

the hair of your head like purple cloth—

a king could be held captive in your tresses.

6 *How beautiful you are and how pleasant,*

O love, with such delights!

Whatever I said and whatever you said, I love you.

The word and the moment forever have fled;
    I love you.
The breezes may ruffle the stream in its flow,
But tranquil and clear are the waters below;
And under all tumult you feel and you know
    I love you.
Whatever I thought and whatever you thought,
    I love you.
The mood and the passion that made it are naught;
    I love you.
For words, thoughts, and deeds,
though they rankle and smart,
May never delude us or hold us apart
Who treasure this talisman deep in the heart:
    "I love you."

Arthur Guiterman

As he becomes speechless, she fills in his missing words. Theirs has become a relationship where they know what the other is thinking.

Man

7 Your stature is like a palm tree;

your breasts are its clusters.

8 I said, "I will climb the palm tree

and take hold of its fruit."

May your breasts be like clusters of grapes,

and the fragrance of your breath like apricots.

9 Your mouth is like fine wine—

Woman

flowing smoothly for my love,

gliding past my lips and teeth!

If ever two were one, then surely we.
If ever man were loved by wife, then thee;
If ever wife was happy in a man,

Compare with me, ye women, if you can.

I prize thy love more than whole mines of gold

Or all the riches that the East doth hold.

My love is such that rivers cannot quench,

Nor ought but love from thee, give recompense.

Thy love is such I can no way repay,

The heavens reward thee manifold, I pray.

Then while we live, in love let's so persevere

That when we live no more, we may live ever.

Anne Bradstreet

The Song of Songs
Chapter 7

No longer cautious of love's commitment, the woman has gained
a maturity and trust that allows her freedom to express herself.

Woman

10 I belong to my love,

and his desire is for me.

11 Come, my love,

let's go to the field;

let's spend the night among the henna blossoms.

12 Let's go early to the vineyards;

let's see if the vine has budded,

if the blossom has opened,

if the pomegranates are in bloom.

There I will give you my love.

The question was asked, "What is the most beautiful view you have ever seen?"

"I think for pure grandeur, I'd take the Swiss Alps."

"The feeling you get in the Colorado Rockies."

"What about Denmark? The countryside, so soft, so soothing. Neat, neat farms; cows grazing."

Then I told them what I was thinking. "For me, the most beautiful sight in all God's creation is Martha—Martha coming down the aisle on Sundays while I sit in my pulpit chair watching the worshipers gather—Martha turning from her stove to smile at me when I tell her I like the aroma of her kitchen—Martha stepping from her shower in the morning."

Charlie Shedd

Sometimes their love will be fresh and surprising; at other times,
unspoken and predictable. There is treasure to be found in both.

Woman

13 The mandrakes give off a fragrance,

and at our doors is every delicacy—

new as well as old.

I have treasured them up for you, my love.

Mighty waters cannot extinguish love,

Chapter 8

Yours Forever

Set me as a seal
on your heart,
as a seal on your arm.
For love is as strong as death.

rivers cannot
sweep it away.

Does my husband know that I protect his reputation by never criticizing him before others? Does he know that even when he fails, I will be there to cushion his fall? Does he know that no matter how harshly he may be treated at work, he can come home to a safe place where he will be loved and appreciated? The partnership of a virtuous woman energizes a man to develop his potential and to assume a place of leadership in whatever arena of life God calls him to serve. Christian men who are supported by wives of noble character can permeate culture with confidence and boldness.

🖋 *Susan Hunt*

Modesty restrains her from hanging on her husband in public. True love doesn't need to be flaunted, for it is its own reward.

Woman

1 *If only I could treat you like my brother,*

one who nursed at my mother's breasts,

I would find you in public and kiss you,

and no one would scorn me.

2 *I would lead you, I would take you,*

to the house of my mother who taught me.

I would give you spiced wine to drink,

and the juice of my pomegranates.

Thou has not that, My child, but thou has Me, and am I not alone enough for thee?

I know it all, know how thy heart was set

Upon this joy which is not given yet.

And well I know how through the wistful days

Thou walkest all the dear familiar ways

As unregarded as a breath of air,

But there in love and longing, always there.

I know it all; but from thy brier shall blow

A rose for others. If it were not so

I would have told thee. Come, then, say to Me,

My Lord, my Love, I am content with Thee.

Amy Carmichael

She had spoken these words earlier, but now she can attest to their wisdom and blessing. Trust me, she says: Love is worth waiting for.

Woman

3 His left hand is under my head,

and his right hand embraces me.

4 Young women of Jerusalem, I charge you:

do not stir up or awaken love

until the appropriate time.

Marriage is not a lifelong attraction of two individuals to each other, but a call for two people to witness together to God's love. The basis for marriage is not mutual affection, or feelings, or emotions and passions that we associate with love, but a vocation, a being elected to build together a house for God in this world, to be like the two cherubs whose outstretched wings sheltered the Ark of the Covenant and created a space where Yahweh could be present. Marriage is a relationship in which a man and a woman protect and nurture the inner sanctum within and between them and witness to that by the way in which they love each other.

Henri Nouwen

At one time, the man had attracted the admiration of the young women. But now, it is the woman—a picture of trust and repose.

Young Women

5 Who is this coming up from the wilderness,

leaning on the one she loves?

Woman

Under the apricot tree I awakened you.

There your mother conceived you;

there she conceived and gave you birth.

This is the anniversary of the day of
days, for us, when we with faith and hope

Fared forth together; solemn and yet gay

We faced the future, for life's upward slope

Was joyous going, and we never thought

Then, that there might be worries—hours of pain

And sleepless nights that left one overwrought—

That loss would often come instead of gain.

But looking back, the time has not seemed long,

Although the road, for us, was sometimes rough.

We have grown quiet, and the buoyant song

Once in our hearts sings low, and yet enough

Of loveliness still lives to make amend

To us, for all the ills life chose to send.

Margaret E. Bruner

How to describe such devotion and commitment? To capture its permanence, she must borrow from terms deeper than life itself.

Woman

6 Set me as a seal on your heart,

as a seal on your arm.

For love is as strong as death;

ardent love is as unrelenting as Sheol.

Love's flames are fiery flames—

the fiercest of all.

7 Mighty waters cannot extinguish love;

rivers cannot sweep it away.

If a man were to give all his wealth for love,

it would be utterly scorned.

Does it do any good to spiritualize about how marriage is like the Christian life

and how true love is God's love? Only if you believe marriage can be a crucial settlement in God's Kingdom. It is exalted, not because it is so different from the rest of life, but because it allows us a frontier to practice God's value system, so that we may derive strength to present that system to the rest of the world. In marriage we are tiptoeing through a field of land mines on the way to paradise. If we succeed—and two do become one—there is no more incredible human relationship. Dostoevski once declared, "I ponder, 'what is hell?' I maintain it is the suffering of being unable to love." What, then, does that make heaven?

Philip Yancey

Others want what this couple has—contentment in a permanent, covenant relationship—for themselves and those they care about.

Brothers

8 Our sister is young: she has no breasts.

What will we do for our sister

on the day she is spoken for?

9 If she is a wall,

we will build a silver parapet on it.

If she is a door,

we will enclose it with cedar planks.

Woman

10 I am a wall and my breasts like towers.

So in his eyes I have become

like one who finds peace.

*From here to there, and then from there
to here, the people of this planet circling roam,*

And I, as well—but, oh, one truth is clear:

I live in God, and God Himself is Home.

From hither and from thither comes the call,

Perhaps to places near, perhaps abroad,

But anywhere I am, and through it all

My heart's at home—for Home is Sovereign God.

To hurry here, and then to scurry there

May be the thing that duty asks of me;

But, oh! my heart is tranquil anywhere,

When God Himself is my Tranquility.

Anne Ortlund

Marriage has brought her a sense of joy and dignity no money can buy—a priceless measure of worth, self-confidence, and identity.

Woman

11 Solomon owned a vineyard in Baal-hamon.

He leased the vineyard to tenants.

Each was to bring for his fruit

a thousand pieces of silver.

12 I have my own vineyard.

The thousand are for you, Solomon,

but two hundred for those who guard its fruits.

The question is asked, "Is anything more beautiful in life than a boy and girl clasping clean hands and pure hearts in the path of marriage?" And the answer is given, "Yes—there is a more beautiful thing; it is the spectacle of an old man and an old woman finishing their journey together on that path. Their hands are gnarled but still clasped; their faces are seamed but still radiant; their hearts are tired and bowed down but still strong. They have proved the happiness of marriage and have vindicated it from the jeers of cynics."

Hymn of Marriage

The man fully realizes how blessed he is, how many others she could have chosen. He needn't worry. She only has eyes for him.

Man

13 You who dwell in the gardens—

companions are listening for your voice—

let me hear you!

Woman

14 Hurry to me, my love,

and be like a gazelle

or a young stag

on the mountains of spices.

Acknowledgments

Page 16: *I Kissed Dating Goodbye* © 1997 Multnomah Press

Pages 22,34,56: *The Mystery of Marriage* © 1985 Multnomah Press

Page 26: *Marriage to a Difficult Man: The Uncommon Union of Jonathan and Sarah Edwards* © 1971 The Westminster Press

Pages 32,84: *Things Pondered* © 1997 Broadman and Holman Publishers

Pages 38,68: *A Man Called Peter: The Story of Peter Marshall* © 1951 McGraw-Hill Book Company

Pages 44,52,82: *Passion and Purity: Bringing Your Love Life Under Christ's Control* © 1984 Fleming H. Revell Company

Pages 46,62: *I John Take Thee Mary: A Book of Christian Marriage* © 1962 Seabury Press

Page 64: *The Mystery of Love and Marriage* © 1952 Harper & Row Publishers

Page 70: *Seduction of the Lesser Gods: Life, Love, Church, and Other Dangerous Idols* © 1997 Word Publishing

Pages 74,118: *Seeds of Hope: A Henri Nouwen Reader* © 1989 Bantam Books

Page 96: *A Search for Serenity: Encouragement for Your Weary Days* © 1990 Multnomah Press

Page 102: *Love That Lasts: Making a Magnificent Marriage* © 1993 People of Destiny International

Page 104: *The Marriage Builder: A Blueprint for Couples and Counselors* © 1982 The Zondervan Corporation

Page 110: *Remember, I Love You: Martha's Story* © 1990 HarperCollins Publishers

Page 114: *By Design: God's Distinctive Calling for Women* © 1994 Crossway Books

Page 122: *After the Wedding* © 1976 Word Publishing

Page 124: *Disciplines of the Beautiful Woman* © 1977 Word Publishing

All other quotes have been taken from anthologies and other available sourcebooks.